Up, Up to the Top

by Rosa Garcia
illustrated by Nathan Jarvis

HOUGHTON MIFFLIN BOSTON

Printed in China

ISBN 10: 0-618-88627-3
ISBN 13: 978-0-618-88627-2

23456789 SDP 16 15 14 13 12 11 10 09 08

I like to play with blocks.
I put my blocks just so.

How many blocks are there?

I get 3 blocks.

I make a bottom row.

Which block is on the left?

I get 2 more blocks.
I make another row.

Which block is in the middle?

I get the last block.
I put it on the top.

Which blocks are below?

I like my pyramid.
It has 3, then 2, then 1.

Which block is above them all?

Oh, they all fall down.
Let's do it again.

Problem Solving

Make a Pyramid

Draw Visualize

1. Draw 3 squares to make a bottom row.
2. Draw 2 squares to make a middle row.
3. Draw 1 square on the top row.

Tell About

1. Tell someone about your picture.
2. Use the words *square*, *top*, *middle*, and *bottom*.

Write

1. Write about your picture.
2. Write the words *square*, *top*, *middle*, and *bottom*.